AUSTRALIAN DIARIES

By Alex Hunter

VAN DIEMEN'S LAND AND TASMANIAN DEVIL PARK

We landed on the island of Tasmania in the middle of the heat wave in summer. Having left one of the coldest European winters behind, it was a temperature shock to adapt from minus 14 degrees Celsius to over 35 degrees Celsius. Sun was shining, skies were bright and blue, and vegetation was green and beautiful. The airport of Hobart is relatively small; it is used for internal flights. People, who come from foreign countries, firstly arrive at the big international airport of Melbourne and then take the plane to Hobart. The airport is guarded by dogs that sniff thoroughly the luggage, searching not only for drugs but for food. It is prohibited to carry any food with you when entering the island. Fruits, vegetables, items made of wood, are prohibited. Any piece of food should be thrown in the rubbish bin before exiting the airport building. Fines are huge for deliberate importation of foreign fruits or vegetables via suitcases. All those rules were made to keep the island from pollution. Tasmania is considered one of the places in the world with the purest waters and cleanest nature. The Government would not allow for foreign types of vegetation to pollute the local flora. It is an important battle because, due to the hundreds thousands years of isolation, the island developed its very own plants and animals. With their close links to the ancient super continent of Gondwana, Tasmania's flora and fauna are unique- here you can discover and observe animals, birds and plants that exist nowhere else on Earth. There are some pre-historic types of vegetation which do not exist anywhere else. In the northwestern part of the islands is situated the largest temperate rainforest area in Australia. Tasmanian rivers were declared to be part of the cleanest rivers in the world. Tasmania is called "The natural state". With such extensive wild natural areas, animals are abundant and often less shy of humans than in more populated regions of mainland Australia. With care, you can get close enough to take some photos of a wild platypus, wombat, kangaroo, rosella or orange-bellied parrot. Most Tasmanian animals are nocturnal- dawn and dusk are the best times to observe them.

Van Diemen's Land was the original name used by the Europeans for the island of Tasmania. The island was discovered by the Dutch explorer Abel Tasman in 1642 who named it. Tasmania is separated from New Zealand by the Tasman Sea and from Australia by the Bass Strait. The island of Tasmania is situated to the south of Australia and it is the natural gateway to the Antarctic.
In the past Tasmania was used as a penal colony for English criminals. Due to the harsh natural and climatic conditions, it was almost impossible for prisoners to escape the colony. In case of a successful escape they were facing big problems- the penal colony was situated on an island, inhabited by unfriendly local tribes, full of unfamiliar animals and unknown plants. The poor runaways were risking their lives to escape only to find themselves in unbearable situation with nothing to eat and nowhere to go. Those facts made from Van Diemen's Land the perfect prison. Nowadays, the historic town of Port Arthur reminds of the severe past of the island.   Port Arthur is one of Australia's most significant heritage areas and an open-air museum. It is located about 97 km south east of Hobart, on the Tasman Peninsula. The scenic drive from Hobart takes around 90 minutes.

Transport from Hobart is also available via bus or ferry, and various companies offer day tours. The peninsula on which Port Arthur is located is a naturally secure site by being surrounded by water. The 30 meters wide isthmus of Eaglehawk Neck that was the only connection to the mainland was fenced and guarded by soldiers, man traps, and half-starved dogs. The prison closed in 1877. Currently the site is preserved as a tourist destination, due to its historical significance.

On the way from Hobart to Port Arthur, at Taranna, is situated the Tasmanian Devil Conservation Park / http://www.tasmaniandevilpark.com /. That is one of the greatest places for visitors where the famous Tasmanian devil can be seen. After leaving the capital city of Hobart, you should drive about two hours towards the Seven Mile Beach and Tasman Peninsula. While driving your car you will pass the historical villages of Richmond, Sorell, Dodges Ferry and Dunnaley and finally reach the Tasmanian Devil Park. The island of Tasmania is famous because of its Tasmanian devils. Thanks to the Warner Bros cartoons, everybody knows the Tasmanian devil- a funny omnivorous animal which is always hungry. In fact, it is a marsupial, feeding on carrion, which resembles a small dog. Its black-and-white fur, big ears and tail make it very attractive for the tourists. Tasmanian devil is the symbol of Tasmania. It is everywhere- in the form of souvenirs, toys, postcards, pictures on T-shirts. This lovely creature was called a "devil" because of its roar which is terrible. The first European settlers of the island had become very scared of this obscure animal, roaring in the deep forests of Tasmania. For the last two centuries millions of devils were killed by the farmers because they blamed them for the death of the sheep. Nowadays, the population of the Tasmanian devil is in danger again because of the skin cancer these animals developed.

The park is open from 9.00 a.m. till 7 p.m. Visitors pay a fee in order to be allowed to enter the park. It is huge, so everybody receives a map at the main reception. On the map are shown all the places of interest, the feeding time of some of the animals / devils, kangaroos, etc. /, the bird shows, some facts about the inhabitants of the park, etc. On entering the park, the first attraction you must see is the movie about the extinct Tasmanian tiger- the so called thylacine. It was the biggest animal in Tasmania, a marsupial with a striped fur. People were afraid of it, hunted and poisoned the thylacine and it is believed to be extinct

at the beginning of the 20th century. The last Tasmanian tiger died in 1936. Although this fact, there are always people who claim that the Tasmanian tiger still lives in the vast wet forests of the Western Tasmania. This is a very shy nocturnal animal so hunters and tourists could see only its footprints. After the video room you enter the real park where the famous Tasmanian devils live. Their cage is very huge- it is surrounded by a thick wall because these tiny animals are very dangerous. They can bite off a human's hand. Their bite is as strong as the bite of a shark. You can take photos, shoot a movie, enjoy their lifestyle, but, please, do not step over the fence. Feeding of the devils is a big attraction. The keepers throw in the cage some kind of offal and the devils start arguing and roaring. The noise is impressive! The devils fight for the meat, run around the cage and pull the carcass. The meal is finished in no time. When there is no meat around them, the Tasmanian devils seem very calm and friendly beings.

A program aiming the protection of the Tasmanian devil exists. It is applied in this park where the sick animals are separated from the healthy ones. The skin cancer spreads very fast because the devils often bite each other. In the park the sick animals are sheltered in separate cages and have no access to the cages of the healthy Tasmanian devils. The program works and lots of devils are set free in the forests in the last years.

Another big attraction in the Tasmanian Devil Park is the place where the kangaroos live. You enter the fence and find yourself surrounded by different kinds of kangaroos- from the tiny wallabies to the huge grey kangaroos. They jump around, play, or just relax under the trees. Tourists have the opportunity to hand-feed them with a special food which the keepers distribute. You can get as much food as you want and spend as much time as you wish feeding the kangaroos. They are very calm and nice marsupials. They eat only grass and corn, so they are not dangerous for humans. You can pet them, feed them, and take photos with them. If you annoy them enough, the kangaroos just move some meters away. Outside the fence live lots of wild wallabies. They come to be fed, too. It may sound strange but the wild kangaroos are not afraid of humans. The time spent in the kangaroos' place can be unforgettable for families with children- kids just enjoy being close to these living plush toys.

Once leaving the kangaroos you are up to find the rich birds' world of Tasmania and Australia. Passing the cages of the wonderful frogmouths, the mighty falcons and eagles, the different kinds of ducks and gooses you will be able to learn about their behavior, diet, and lifestyle.

The show with the birds of prey is another amazing attraction you should not miss. Falcons are the stars there. They are trained in an excellent way and the visitors can see falcons in fly, grabbing their prey, etc. These beautiful birds leave indelible impression.

The tour around the park finishes at the point it has started - in the reception area where the tourists can find lots of souvenirs, pictures and postcards. The day spent in the Tasmanian Devil Park is a wonderful way to make you familiar with the amazing wildlife of Tasmania - the last paradise on Earth.

Alex Hunter

SCHOOLS

The Australian education system is very different from most European systems. In Australia, the school year starts in mid-February / the exact day is different across different states, but the difference consists of only a few days / and ends in mid-December. There are three school terms with small breaks after each. At the end of each term, parents receive a school report on their child's successes and failures. Its volume is about 2 large pages and it details the achievements and problems of the student. In this way, each parent receives feedback from the school and can track their child's development.

Children start first grade when they are six years old. Before that, there is one year of pre-school preparation. There are no kindergartens similar to those in many countries in Europe. At the age of four children start attending kindergarten at school, but only twice a week for few hours. In this way, they are considered to be accustomed to the situation and are expected to have no problems when they start the primary school. The lack of public kindergartens puts parents in a situation where they either have to hire a babysitter or the mother has to stay at home until the child starts school. In general, wages are calculated in such manner that one working parent is able to cover all the family expenses. Lower-income families also receive various benefits from the state. There are private children's playrooms, which are quite expensive. It is very difficult for parents to find a vacant place because there are many candidates. These are the so-called ABC centers. In Tasmania, they had decided to close some of these centers and the newspapers were filled with angry letters from parents. It is difficult to find a babysitter. To work as a babysitter, you must equip yourself with at least three recommendations from previous employers, a state driver's license, a first aid certificate, a certificate or a diploma in childcare. It is almost impossible for an immigrant to start such a job (unlike in the European countries), because it will be very difficult to get the whole set of documents.

When children are at school, parents, and especially mothers, become actively involved in school life. There are often school celebrations, school fairs, etc. The main purpose is to raise funds for the school. Several times during the year, sales of clothes, toys, books, discs, etc. are organized in the school itself. Each parent receives one sack from the school, which is desirable to be filled with unnecessary items in good condition. The sales are organized very carefully and attract great public interest. They are announced several weeks in advance around the neighborhood and are one of the local attractions for residents. Parents of children from each class prepare together various treats to sell at the fair, raffles with prizes, racing games for the kids with prizes. Early in the morning, music from the school invites the visitors. School sales and fairs are a welcome and anticipated event for children and parents. They are also an interesting and completely legal way to raise money, which is used after that to buy the necessary books, materials, equipment for the school.

Public school education is free. In the beginning of the year, a fee of about $ 200 is collected to cover the cost of school trips and outings throughout the school year. There are also private schools, most of them Catholic. I was told that regarding the primary education it does not matter whether the children are enrolled in a state or a Catholic school - they will receive the same education. The difference is in the high school training – the curriculum in Catholic schools is more serious, the discipline is stricter and there is more homework to be completed. However, regardless of whether they receive their education in a public or a private school, all students can enroll in a university if they wish. Many young Australians do not consider university a compulsory continuation of their education, and a relatively small proportion of them continue studying after high school.

School uniforms are obligatory. However, these are some very practical and comfortable outfits that have nothing to do with the designer models of the British schools. The uniform at my daughter's school - Albuera Street School - was the following: a yellow short-sleeved T-shirt with the school logo, dark shorts, dark ankle-length sports trousers, blue jumper with the school logo, and blue polar sweater for the winter and the compulsory sun hat for the spring and summer. For the girls, there was also available a blue and white checkered dress to wear instead of shorts. No special school shoes were required; kids were wearing their own most comfortable shoes. Actually, primary school students spend the whole day in the room without shoes. They take them off when enter the room and can sit comfortably on the floor in a clean environment. We bought a second-hand uniform from the school few days before the start of the school year, which cost about 15 AUD. Prices for new uniforms are much higher. We paid the entire price of 45 AUD only for the polar sweater because it was ordered separately before the start of the Tasmanian winter. This type of uniform is really quite functional, does not restrict the movement of children, does not squat, does not need ironing, and dries quickly after washing. I definitely do not like the uniforms with white shirts, ties, and other restricting accessories. It seems that the Australian schools have solved the problem with uniforms – their uniforms are comfortable and decent looking for everyone.

Primary education is limited to a few subjects: English, Mathematics, Music, Arts and much of sport. In the third grade children begin to study one foreign language- mostly French, but at a very low level. Since the beginning of fourth grade, they are also trained to play a musical instrument: guitar, for example. Separately, there are special English classes for immigrant children only, and a special teacher is appointed to teach them, usually twice a week.

In primary schools students have no textbooks. At the beginning of the school year, they are handed a notebook for the school subject where they write, paste, and draw. The notebooks are kept in school, but I have asked every Friday to bring them home so I can monitor the child's development and help where necessary. In third grade, they were still writing with a black pencil to be able to correct their mistakes. My daughter was very happy when she received a certificate during the second term, which gave her the right to write with a pen - only a few children had acquired a similar privilege by the end of the school year.

Sport is the most emphasized school subject in primary schools. There is at least one hour for sport every day. Children run, jump, play different games. This is one of the big differences between British and European primary schools and Australian primary schools. The school's sports facilities are maintained in perfect condition. Children get used to moving. My daughter had big problems in the beginning. During the first month at school he constantly complained of muscle fever, stumbling, falling, and lack of endurance when running long distances. For about a month, she got used to the intense sports activities, lost weight, started running fast, competing, and then she was included in the running and football teams. Australians are big fans of sport and school is no exception. To develop correctly, children need to move enough. Instead of overloading them with study items, more time is devoted to sports. At the moment, I am following with interest the efforts of the Government to tackle the problem with overweight in children by imposing food restriction and taxes on sugary drinks. In my opinion, this is the wrong way. In Australia I could not see foods restricted in any way, but very few children were overweight. They bring packed lunch at school - mostly sandwiches, cupcakes, chips, waffles, soups, etc. There is no limit to the amount - they eat as much as they want. Overweight is controlled through sports activities - calories consumed are burned during the daily sports activities. If we want our children to develop in a normal way, we must first think about sports facilities in schools. There is no need for very expensive repairs and expensive equipment - the availability of sports fields, balls, basketball courts, football, volleyball and a sharp increase in physical education hours would be enough. It is necessary for at least one hour a day for the children to have the opportunity for active sports activity, to participate in different sports teams and in competitions. Of course, the number of qualified sports teachers should also increase.

One of the most shocking things for me on my first visit to school was the complete lack of noise, screams, bumps along the corridors, etc. The school building was full of order; the students were extremely disciplined and, from a very young age, they have been brought up to speak quietly, to be kind and polite to their classmates and to adults. Teachers do not raise their voices, nobody screams, they all relate culturally to one another. In the beginning it was a big problem for my daughter. She is a shy and quiet student but for Australian school standards she appeared to be an aggressive and noisy child. She was trying to resolve disputes on her own, sometimes with tougher actions (pushing, yelling, etc. We had to somehow teach her that disputes were resolved with courtesy, and with every problem the children had to seek the assistance of the teacher. The transition from her old school reality to the Australian school in the first few months was very difficult. A year later, when we got back, we had to make the same transition again - this time in the opposite version - to get her used to dealing with aggression and noise at school.

CLIMATE

The climate in Tasmania is just like the English climate. In summer, temperatures do not exceed 30 degrees Celsius, with most days being around 20-22 degrees Celsius. It often rains. In winter, temperatures rarely fall below 8-9 degrees Celsius. Snow does not fall in Hobart. The surrounding peaks, however, get covered with snow. Mount Wellington looks very beautiful with a snow coat. The Tasmanian climate does not change sharply; there are no sudden colds or a temperature difference of more than 10 degrees. In winter and summer, it is good to have a sweater and umbrella with you. Sudden rains, followed by hot sun, make the sweater, the T-shirt under it and the umbrella much needed. In Hobart, within a few hours, the weather can change repeatedly - from sunny to rainy, then the sunny again, at some time a strong wind begins to blow, which brings new rain. Due to its climate, Tasmania is called the "green state" or "natural state" of Australia. Unlike the continent's climate, in the summer Tasmania is a haven for tourists trying to escape from the heat of their hometown. I did not have the chance to survive a true Tasmanian winter. I spent the winter up North, in hot Port Hedland, and learnt about the snow on the peaks and the rains from the photos and picture postcards.

There is an ozone hole above Tasmania. Because of this, sun-protective clothing for children is mandatory, and for adults is recommended.

Tasmania is also famous for being the state with the cleanest air and the cleanest water in the world. The tap water is ideal for drinking; the air is fresh and clean. I usually suffer from hay fever in Europe during the spring, but in Tasmania it did not start – most probably, because of the different types of plants. In the Tasmanian rivers there is no silt because there are no organisms that form it. The Tasmanians keep their nature clean, the quarantine areas are formed at the airports, and the import of fruits, vegetables, seeds, woody wood is not allowed to avoid contamination and the introduction of organisms that are not native to the local people. However, sometimes violators slip. Currently, the state is fighting foxes - non-native animals that kill native fauna and disturb the natural balance.

In north-western Australia the climate conditions are very different from the Tasmanian weather. I arrived in Port Hedland on May 25th. I departed from Hobart wearing a long sleeved jumper, a jacket, freezing in the cold at six in the morning. On the plane from Perth to Port Hedland, I took off my jacket, then my long-sleeved jumper. When I arrived, I was wearing just a T-shirt and long trousers, but it was still too hot for me. I quickly learned that in the winter, daytime temperatures in northwestern Australia are about 35 degrees Celsius. They fall sharply at night because of the desert climate and I was often finding myself twisting with two blankets at night and still getting cold. During the winter in Port Hedland, it rains two or three times. I was told that in summer the temperatures reach 55 degrees Celsius - impossible for me, as European, to survive. I spent winter and spring in Port Hedland. In the spring, the temperatures and humidity began to gradually increase, it was becoming more difficult to breathe, and the season of unpleasant insects began. Coming out of my room, I found it difficult to breathe because of the high humidity. In Europe, we are not used to such type of climate and we can hardly imagine it. I was trying to catch my breath - as if something was burning in my throat. My Australian friends told me that they could not imagine how I would survive in summer when the temperature and humidity would get even higher. In fact, I didn't stay for the summer in the Northwest. I left Port Hedland with temperatures of about 45 degrees Celsius and high humidity. I can only try to imagine how the summer season is- ten degrees hotter and much wetter.

In winter in northwestern Australia the climate is tolerable with low humidity, with temperatures like in Southern Europe during the summer. The Europeans are not used to the harsh Australian climate in the summer. After a 5-minute walk under the sun without a hat, I was severely hit by sunstroke. Then they told me that I had been very stupid because I had gone outside without putting a hat on my head.

Overall, in Australia, the southern, south-eastern and south-western parts are favorable areas to live. The further north someone goes, the worse the weather becomes. Humidity rises, and so does the temperatures. Australia's sun shines very strongly - you can literally feel it burning your skin. Therefore, the mandatory clothes for employees are the long-sleeved shirts and long trousers. During the summer, a hat is a must-have accessory. However, the fifth continent leads the world ranking in skin cancer. There are videos on the television persuading the population to wear protective clothing, and in schools hats are obligatory.

ALCOHOL

Pilbara is prohibited by law from serving pure alcohol in establishments. Solid alcohol must be mixed with a soft drink and then served. This law is passed because of workers who should not get drunk to a condition where they cannot go to work in the morning and because of the local aboriginal people. Mining companies prohibit their workers from drinking more than a glass or two of alcohol a week. In the morning, when they go to work, they are randomly checked with a breathalyzer for alcohol and if someone is not sober from the previous night, he may lose his job. Therefore, during the weekdays, the bars are quiet, but on Saturday nights there is no free space - everyone drinks because Sunday is a day off and they will be able to get sober till Monday.
The second reason for the legislation, the aboriginal people, cannot absorb drink. They get drunk from small quantities. According to the law, establishments cannot refuse the indigenous people to come in and drink beer or something stronger. According to the internal rules of bars, bartenders are obliged to refuse the sale of alcohol to intoxicated persons. It is difficult to enforce these rules though, as scandals immediately begin.

In general, the bar is the major attraction of the small Australian places. There were several main bars in Port Hedland and one of them was the bar of our hotel. People from all over the area were coming there. Immediately, after finishing work, as a rule, people were going to the bar. For several months, the bar became my second home, too.

It was much cheaper to buy alcohol from the store instead of drinking in the bar. It should be noted that in Australia, alcohol is only sold in special liquor stores called Bottle shops. You cannot even find beer in supermarkets and convenience stores. This was something very strange for a European immigrant. I remember when I decided to buy some beer in Tasmania for the first time. Of course, the most logical thing was to go into one of the big supermarkets and have a look. My surprise came after half an hour of searching when I was able to find only some ginger beer, which later turned out to be a sweet soft drink. After that I was told that beer can only be found in specialized stores. The beer and the all types of alcohols were so expensive that all the pleasure disappeared somewhere. Perhaps the high prices of the alcohol are one of the ways to combat alcoholism that Australians have successfully introduced.

It is forbidden for persons under the age of 18 to enter places where alcohol is served or sold and this prohibition is strictly observed. The fines for its violation are enormous. If the family wants to buy alcohol, one of the parents enters the store and the other stays outside with the kids. Children have no right to enter such a place at all. Therefore, a family with children cannot rent a room in a hostel, for example - the hostels are allowed to sell alcohol, so children have no place there.

IMMIGRANTS IN AUSTRALIA

Australian Government has developed a strict points system for immigration. There are many different types of visas which depend on the points the immigration applicant would be able to collect. Points depend on age, education, professional skills, work experience, knowledge of English and community languages /as community languages are considered all the languages spoken in the immigrant diasporas and may be European languages, Asian languages, African languages, etc./. In that way the Government aims to guarantee that Australia would attract the most skilled professional people from around the world, young enough to integrate and to raise their children in the new country.

The Australian Government's new policy is aimed at Asia. The distant goal is to make Australia part of the Asian continent. Currently, the Australian football team is competing in the Zone of Asia in the World Cup qualifiers and the main flow of foreign trade is to China and Japan. Nowadays there are many immigrants from Asia in Australia. Till 1979 it was forbidden for Asian immigrants to settle on Australian soil. After the repeal of the law, things have changed and now half of Australians were actually born in an Asian country.

Immigrants from Asia get visas and jobs relatively easily. There are intergovernmental programs with the Philippines, for example, according to which the citizens of this country can get a job in Australia. Asian families are big, but Australia is big as well. The fact that most of the territory of the country is practically uninhabited does not prevent immigrants from settling in the large metropolitan areas and to remain there.
Asian languages - mainly Japanese, Chinese and Indonesian - are taught in many high schools, colleges and universities. These are the foreign languages young Australians want to learn. Asia is a promising and closer trade partner than Europe.

Due to the proximity of the Asian continent, boats full of immigrants are constantly trying to reach Australia. Border control is rigorous, but some boats still manage to reach their desired destination. In the past, on the Australian territory there were detention centers for illegal immigrants. Even in Port Hedland, there was a similar center that has been turned afterwards into a workers' camp by some mining companies. Nowadays, illegal immigrants arriving by boats from Asia are sent to Nauru Island or some other Australian islands without the chance to step on the territory of the fifth continent at all. Despite the facilitation of visa requirements for Asian countries, the flow of illegal immigrants is not discontinuing.

Europeans in Australia had come from all countries of the old continent. Most are English, Germans, Italians, Greeks and maybe French. Many of them are old immigrants - 50-60 years ago or second and third generation. The Greek Diaspora is everywhere – it also exists in Tasmania. You can enjoy delicious souvlaki, moussaka, baklava at one of the many Greek fast food establishments. Every year, a Greek festival takes place in Hobart during the Greek week. Similar Greek colonies are scattered throughout the continent. The situation is the same with the Italians. Bulgarian migrants are mainly targeting the East Coast and major cities such as Sydney, Melbourne, Brisbane, and Adelaide.

AUSTRALIAN WAY OF WORK

Looking for a job in Australia is a complicated mission. Before leaving for the fifth continent we prepared all the possible diplomas and certificates that we had from the schools, universities and other educational institutions we had graduated, translated into English, with the corresponding signatures, stamps, etc. Some of the diplomas were previously recognized to meet the Australian educational requirements because without that recognition it is almost impossible to collect the necessary points for an immigrant visa. Full with optimism for a bright professional future, we started our search for any kind of job. It turned out to be far from the simple job search in European countries. In Australia, there is a complex system of certificates, diplomas, and licenses. Each state has its own requirements for diplomas and certificates; therefore we had to equate our previously recognized diplomas with the educational requirements of Tasmania. One big problem in Australia and in Tasmania in particular, is that you have to look for a job based on your education. There are numerous job agencies where everyone can register for free and wait for them to find the most suitable job. Their first question was always: "What education and profession do you have?" When they heard the answer: "Electrician", they started looking only for a job positions for an electrician. However, if a foreigner wants to work in this professional field in Tasmania, he/ she must obtain a Tasmanian license. There are separate licenses for each state - a license for Victoria, for Western Australia, for Queensland, etc. This license is very difficult to be obtained. Australians do not recognize the specialties related to the electricity, respectively internships, outside Australia. The only exception is for the citizens of New Zealand because their system of licenses and certificates is the same as the Australian system. In general, New Zealand and Australia do mutually recognize their educational and professional qualifications and any person who has completed his/ her education or an internship in New Zealand can easily find a job in the same specialty in any Australian state.

We were forced to develop fake CVs for each position we were applying for, stating that we had a lot of experience. For example, if you are applying for the position of a shop assistant, you cannot write that you have got a college degree because you will be immediately told that you are overqualified. Perhaps, that was one of the reasons I could not find a job for a few months - I seemed overqualified even with a fake CV. If a foreigner wants to qualify for a particular specialty, the best advice would be to study at TAFE, a post-secondary vocational education institution, and to pass the exams. As newcomers, we could not afford to pay tuition fees or stay out of work. With our type of visa, for the first two years we were not entitled to social security benefits or inclusion in the Australian state health insurance system. Therefore we needed to find some job.

A few months later, that circumstance sent me to North-Western Australia, to the Walkabout Motel in Port Hedland, Pilbara. I read in the local newspaper the announcement that the hotel was looking for people to work at the reception desk. Usually, when I was applying for the jobs listed in the newspaper, I was never receiving any response from the employers or I was receiving only rejections. My optimism had dropped below zero but I continued to stubbornly send CVs and one day I received a phone call from the reception manager at the Walkabout Motel in Port Hedland, who invited me for an interview. We met at the Starbucks Café in downtown Hobart and talked for about an hour and a half. One of the important questions at the interview was about my survival skills in an isolated place outside the small town.

At the end of the interview, Karen, the manager, told me, "We will call you these days for the result," and once again my confidence sank. I really hate the phrase: "We will call you". From my experience, they would never call again. It is just a polite way to end the conversation. However, I received a phone call late in the evening and was told that I got the job and had to fly to Port Hedland as soon as possible. The flight from Hobart to Port Hedland took 14 hours, with change of flights in Melbourne and Perth.

Employees at the hotel were getting a free plane ticket which price was subsequently deducted from their pay. However, if a person was stubborn enough to work there for three months, the ticket money was given back. This term became my goal. I was determined to get my ticket money back (worth about 1,000 AUD).

Wild capitalism ruled at work in Pilbara. They hired me to work at the reception desk and in a very short time I learnt the computer reservation program and became a professional. I should mention that I have never worked as a receptionist in my life. My idea of the front desk has always been from the perspective of the tourist. However, I was good with computers and quickly learnt what to do. In case of a problem, I was explaining that we were doing things differently in Europe and I was getting out of the situation. My work day at the front desk was 8 hours long and the salary was 20 AUD per hour. However, 29% of those 20 AUD was going for taxes. Those were the taxes for the Australian citizens and holders of particular visa types. If I had to pay taxes as a foreigner, then half my salary would be deducted – foreigners were paying 49% for taxes. The hotel accountant explained a lot to me about taxation in Australia. Almost all the hotel staff was receiving the same salary of 20 AUD per hour. Only the managers of different departments: reception, kitchen, cleaning, bar were receiving higher salaries, but they were working on contract while the rest of the staff was paid per hour. Chefs also had higher salaries because finding a good chef was a widespread problem in Australia. Apart from the 8 hours at the reception desk, I had the right to work more hours elsewhere in the hotel. I started doing some cleaning duties and some work at the restaurant and kitchen and my salary became higher. The multiple jobs were saving my mind from the loneliness, as there was nothing to do during the days off. There were several options for leisure time activities: drinking in the bar, watching TV in the room / nothing interesting though /, reading books, drinking beer outside in the yard, sleeping or shopping with co-workers in the supermarkets in Port Hedland or South Hedland /organized activity because everyone was going by the bus of the hotel/.

In order to not lose my mind, I preferred to work. I was supporting a family in Hobart and also wanted to save as much money as possible. I was earning over 1,000 AUD per week at my abnormal work timetable. I was taking one day off every 3 weeks, which was absolutely illegal, but in the wild northwest labor legislation was not observed very strictly. My only fear was to not get sick. There was no paid sick leave and if you were sick you had to rest without getting paid. You also might be directly sacked because of your illness. One of the restaurant chefs had cut his hand deeply to the bone. He had a rest for a day and then started working with a bandage and glove. He said that if he gave himself a few more days off sick, he would have to look for another job. In Pilbara you can understand that there are no irreplaceable people. Everyone is just a bolt in the machine - if the person breaks down, another one will be found. The staff was not staying too long at the hotel, but the bosses were worrying because new job applicants were coming in every day. There also were some prominent lazy workers who were waiting for the others to do their job. However, we were not complaining because we could be thrown away. While you were healthy and able to work, you were welcome in the hotel. In case of sickness you had to survive alone. The law of the jungle reigned in full force.

Work in Australia, and almost all over the world, is largely automated. People needed to perform certain actions for a certain period of time. Independent thinking is not tolerated: instructions have been created for the purpose to be followed. In this way working people are becoming robots. The economy needed workers- bolts in the big machine. I can give an example with myself: in about one week time my movements got automated to the point where I already knew what I was going to do every minute. Of course, I was not obliged to follow this murderous rhythm of work, but given that I had a family to support and wanted to save money, I had no choice. When managers were asking me how I was able to work so many hours without a day off, I was telling them that I was stubborn enough.

Trade unions in North-Western Australia played no role. Workers definitely did not know their rights. There was no one to protect them in case of illness or any other problems. I was told that there possibly were trade unions in Perth, but no one knew their co-ordinates. This was a big surprise for me, as I was accustomed to the idea that the role of trade unions is important for workers. I was surprised to see that the Australian workers were not counting on any assistance from trade unions in case of problems at work place. Usually people were saying: "If the manager says so, you need to either obey or leave." A third option was not in their imagination.

Perhaps this perception of things was dictated by the fact that Australia is a really large country. Many Australians lead a nomadic lifestyle. They tour the continents with caravans, live in caravan parks and look for temporary jobs only. When they dislike one place, they move to another. The immensity of the fifth continent has influenced the thinking and mentality of its inhabitants. Australians work quietly, do not strive to prove themselves, calculate their time in an optimal way, so that they can get the maximum pay with minimum efforts. They do not stay at the same workplace for a long time. I would like to emphasize again that I am talking mainly about the Northwest and the low-skilled jobs. Of course, no Australian at a senior management position or in a skilled work would afford to change jobs every month. The people I had the opportunity to communicate with originated from the Australian lower class. Without big ambitions or high level of education, these contemporary nomads were touring the continent in search of something better. Sometimes in the evening we would walk around the park and were dreaming of getting a caravan to travel with. When you move, you have a lot more opportunities in front of you. You can even go to Queensland - the dream of many people from Western Australia. About this East Coast state, I have only listened to superlatives. According to my co-workers, it was Australia's most beautiful place, with the best job opportunities and highest pay. I cannot say how many of those tales were reflecting the reality and how many of them were urban legends. I did not travel to Queensland during my first stay on the continent (maybe next time I will go there first), but the fact is that it was kind of Promised Land for my friends from the west.

In Western Australia, the highest paid job was in the mines or as a truck driver. Surprisingly, women were preferred as truck drivers. According to Australian employers, they were calmer and more responsible. Therefore, a female driver had the chance a very well-paid job. Of course, this is also a very tiring and difficult job, but the money is worth it. The truck drivers in Port Hedland were earning about between 7000 AUD and 8000 AUD per week. Working hours, however, were 12 hours a day, Monday to Saturday, inclusive. With luck, you would be able to arrange to work on Sundays when the pay was double. There was the opportunity for drivers with foreign driving licenses to start work at a lower salary (still much better than the salary of low-skilled workers), as an apprentice, and after a year to get a full driving license.

In Northwestern Australia / Pilbara and Kimberly / wages were the highest. The pay depended on the state, the existing work and the staff available. The hourly rate for the lowest paid work in Pilbara was 20 AUD. Employers were not entitled to pay less than the statutory wages and were not entitled to delay any payments. The system of licenses and diplomas largely limits the opportunities for people to change their field of professional activity. If someone was trained as a baker, it would be very difficult for him/her to become an electrician, for example. This system is a knife with two blades. On one hand, it gives a profession to people, with strictly regulated rules and provides confidence to future employers that they would be able to find qualified staff. On the other hand, it partly enslaves people and prevents them from easily changing their profession. In my professional life for over than 20 years I have often been changing my occupation, the fields of activity as I have constantly been striving for improvement and new chances. The fact that everyone should do the job for which has obtained a degree, regardless of skills, aspirations and talents, seemed extremely limiting to me. Perhaps this is one of the reasons why young Australians are reluctant to continue their education at university immediately after graduating from high school, and prefer to travel the country for a few years trying out many unskilled jobs while trying to decide what they would actually like to do. Two-thirds of the employees at the hotel were exactly that kind of young people, who were not staying in one place, were travelling a lot, meeting people, trying to live independently from family and school, so that they could one day decide what they would like to do during the rest of their lives.

THE OUTBACK

There is an expression in Australian English: "The Outback". It characterizes the vast territories outside of Australia's major cities. Outback is the real Australia - the one we know from movies and books. This is the red Australia, covered with low shrubby vegetation, burnt by the sun. Roads in the wilderness are mostly unpaved, red rather than black. The view from the air resembles the surface of the planet Mars. The Red Desert stretches as far as the view goes. Fires are raging at some places all year round. Low vegetation burns. The fire never spreads over vast territory, but moves. When the vegetation burns in one place, the fire goes in the other direction, and new bushes grow in the place of the bushes that were swallowed by the fire. The fires serve to nourish the sandy soil in a natural way and enable the emergence of new vegetation, just as tough and durable as its predecessors.

Contrary to wilderness perceptions, the Australian outback is full of life. It is the territory of the most poisonous snakes on earth, of many different species of reptiles, the main food of which are snakes, of swarms of insects - more or less visible, terrorizing travelers with their constant bites. Many large mammals such as the kangaroos, for example, consider the outback their home.

Camels are newcomers to the Australian desert. They were imported in the middle and late 19th century and were breeding without control. The initial task of the camels was extremely important - in an area where water was more expensive than gold, camels were used to transport cargo, to dig wells, and to provide animal power in deep drillings in the deserts. With the help of camels, the continent was crossed for the first time from south to north and from east to west. The great Australian travelers and discoverers of the late 19th and early 20th centuries had placed all their hopes on the endurance of the Arabian camels in the desert regions and camels had not betrayed them. Some Aboriginal tribes are also accustomed to using camels for transport across their native desert places. At present, however, the uncontrolled breeding of those large mammals puts the Australian Government in front of difficult problems to solve. Camels destroy the scarce desert vegetation and thus deprive other native Australian animals of their food. While we were living in Australia, a newspaper campaign was launched to advertise the usefulness of camel meat - the natural solution to the problem would be a controlled culling of the animals imported from outside. The purpose of the government is not to kill all the camels, but to reduce their populations. However, for this measure to have an effect, people have to get used to eat camel meat. This would have a dual effect - diversifying the menu and controlling the camel herds.

Other huge inhabitants of the outback are the Australian cattle. These are semi-wild black bulls and cows. Some of the herds belong to the local Aboriginal communities; others are free inhabitants of the outback. These cattle strive for places with water and on several occasions at our hotel we have had some exemplars sneaking into its territory. Different lizards are the most common animals in the wilderness, along with snakes. Their varieties are thousands, from tiny insectivorous lizards, through small dinosaur-like lizards which run on their two rear legs, to iguanas and huge lizards that feed on snakes. Wherever those huge lizards appear, the snakes disappear. Various types of snakes live in the outback, including some of the most venomous snakes in the world, named "King Brown". Human may die from a snake bite in the vast outback territories. The distances between towns and populated places are so long, that it may take much of time to reach a hospital. All the tourists are warned to make as much noise as possible when walking, because in that way they would scare the snakes around. However, if you see a snake close to you, you should not move. If you stay still without moving, the snake will just pass around and go away. Making movements can be extremely dangerous and life-threatening. The snake would accept movements as an attack and would bite. Of course, some of the

snakes in the Australian outback are not poisonous. Large py-
thons live there, they look scary because of their dimensions but
they are not life-threatening.

The Outback sun is very strong and burning. The incessant wild-
fires of the desert are caused by its burning rays. Sandstorms are
another big problem. While I was working at the hotel, I experi-
enced a similar sandstorm. In a very short time the wind carried
tons of sand through the air and visibility became zero. It was not
visible beyond a meter. The sand was everywhere - in the eyes,
nose, mouth, ears. For the first time in my life I witnessed such
a sandstorm. It was dark outside, as if it was not lunch time but
evening. The storm lasted for about an hour. Outside, everything
was covered by fine red sand - cars were buried under the sand,
sand rugs were laid in the rooms and corridors. Such sandstorms
were common in the area, as local people told me, and were hap-
pening several times a year.

Other dangerous visitors of the Australian Northwestern coast
are the typhoons. Port Hedland has been destroyed several times
by typhoons. When I arrived in Pilbara for the first time, I was
warned of that danger. There are warning codes for the population in several colors - blue, yellow, red. When the warning code is
yellow, people should start collecting their most important pos-

sessions in a small travel bag to take with them in case of a red code. If the code is red, the typhoon is inevitable and everyone should go to the hiding places in the town. Those hiding places are stable structures with a stable roofs and walls. Luckily, I did not experience a typhoon because I left Port Hedland at the start of the summer season, which is also the hurricane season.

I love the Australian outback, despite its harsh climate conditions, lots of nasty insects and venomous snakes and despite the sandstorms. This is a wonderful place where real people live, unspoiled by civilization. They live by their own rules, have a very strong sense of justice and can be loyal friends. The difficult way of living has taught them to help the people around them, to not try in a fraudulent way to obtain any goods that would not be of great benefit for them. In the outback money is not the most important thing. There are more important things for its inhabitants- to remain human beings, to survive in adverse conditions, to help a person in need. Of course, people of the other type also can be met - greedy, irresponsible, and lazy. However, these are not the true inhabitants of the Northwest. The locals distinguish themselves from them, they call them fools. No one is stronger and greater than the outback from their point of view. A person must live in harmony with himself/herself and the others. My real friends turned out to be the old residents of the outback. I had never, anywhere, felt as well protected as there, at the end of the world. Their philosophy was that people should be proud of the work they do, work in such a way that they feel satisfied with the work done. Money, nice clothes, gold are all transient things that you cannot take with you. Decent lives, willingness to help the people around you, a good job, however, are those things that can show what kind of person you really are. When they accepted me into their hearts, I felt incredible pride and joy. People of the outback do not easily accept strangers. They are as harsh as the nature where they live. More than 100 years ago, Australian adventurers began settling on those wild land and raising families there. They had resisted the prolonged droughts, typhoons, fires, and today their descendants are considered the salt of the Australian lands - proud, independent, and honest.

Pilbara is a vast territory in the state of Western Australia, covered by red sand. It is low-populated and nowadays is considered one of the best places to work because of the high salaries. However, it was not a rich place in the past and people were struggling to live there. That made them resistant and strong and taught them to appreciate the little things. Port Hedland was established in the second part of the 19th century and was destroyed several times by typhoons. However, people were rebuilding it again and again.

The world's longest train runs in Pilbara. Its length is between 2 and 3 kilometers and is loaded with iron ore. If you happen to wait for the train to pass, you have to be very patient - the waiting time is at least 10 minutes until the endless line of wagons continues its way. The long trains are the property of the BHP Company, which owns the largest iron mines.

Pilbara and Northwestern Australia are famous for their numerous iron ore, manganese and salt mines. Port Hedland is Australia's largest industrial port because of mines. The biggest attraction in the city is the tour of the mines of BHP. The tour is by bus, which does not allow tourists to get off while they are on the territory of that big mining company. Tourists can take pictures through the windows of the bus, tour around mountains of iron ore; look at the loading of the train and unloading it on the ships in the harbor.

Salt mines are another attraction around Port Hedland. Salty hills rise in the sunshine- white and beautiful as snow-drifts. They are surrounded by vast salt lakes, from which the salt is extracted. There is an iron sculpture in one of these salt lakes: the hand of a drowning person surrounded by shark fins.

The Aboriginal people have lived in Pilbara for 50,00 years before the European colonisation of the region. The early history of the first peoples is held within an oral tradition, archeological evidence and petroglyphs.

Many Aborigines still live on the continent. They are divided into different tribes, who had fought each other for centuries. Extensive territories, mostly desert areas, are given to the indigenous people - these are their lands, not Australian ones. In the Northern Territory, east of the state capital, the city of Darwin, extends the vast land of the Arnhem people. In central Australia, in the deserts, there are large lands that have always been home to indigenous people. Aboriginal territories are under the responsibility of special governmental offices, and doctors, teachers and other professionals are appointed there. Often, the salaries of the people hired to work there are higher. Many things are being done about health, education, the integration of indigenous people.

After two centuries of isolation, they are once again full residents of their own country. Because of the 200-year genocide against the indigenous people, the government feels guilty these days. The Prime Minister formally apologized to the Aborigines for the fact that white settlers from the late 18th century to the end of the 20th century pursued a very discriminatory policy against them. Celebrations were shown on television in honor of the Prime Minister's words.

Aboriginal families often live under a tree in the outback. Trees in the Australian wilderness are rare but huge, keeping a wide shade. Below them usually lives a family of 10-15 people. This has been their way of life for 50 millennia and it would be very unrealistic to expect from them to change in a few years. These are the only people who can survive in the harsh climatic conditions of the Australian deserts without the benefits of civilization. In the extremely dry climate of northwestern Australia, they can always find water, food, shade. Australia's sun is merciless, but native indigenous people walk without hats, naked, barefoot /on the scorched earth /. The Australian wilderness is not a real desert, as it is mistakenly believed. Red sands are dotted with thickly growing shrubs- the so-called bush. It is resilient, thorny vegetation, extremely unpleasant for barefoot walking. In addition, the bush is full of poisonous snakes and insects. Aboriginal people are perfectly suited to this harsh nature where the European settlers had not been able to endure for a long time. By the way, the area where Port Hedland was built is called "Good Water" in the local Aboriginal language. Where they would find the water I could only guess. The city is currently supplied with purified seawater that is not good for drinking. Therefore, the bottled water industry is booming, and bottled water itself is sold at a relatively expensive price.

Alex Hunter

To some extent the native indigenous people of Australia have the right to expect compensations for their suffering in the past. They were slaughtered for two hundred years by the European settlers, they had no rights at all, and their children were taken away to study in special schools. The expression of "The lost generation" characterizes the cruel policies of new settlers who were violent towards the Aboriginal children and trained them for servants and cleaners, thousands of miles away from their families. In this way, children had forgotten their native languages, their traditions, and their history, lost their identity and formed the lowest stratum of society. The lost generation is a broken thread of the indigenous culture. Whole tribes disappeared from the face of the earth along with their culture and languages while their children were imprisoned in special schools. Many movies have been made regarding this tragic period of Australian history; one of the most emotional ever is "Rabbit Fence".

Aboriginal people in the wilderness still live in the era of dreams.

However, very few of Australia's indigenous peoples have been left untouched by the vices of civilization. Much of their knowledge related to the world, nature, land where they live has already been lost. The inability to pass on their knowledge to the children who come after them, the desire of young people to live in cities, the declining number of tribes are factors that contribute to the loss of knowledge and skills acquired throughout their millennial history. Their myths and legends are collected in books, but young people do not know what is told in them. Hopefully, one day the rich heritage of Aboriginal people in Australia will be fully revived and people will learn about those indigenous traditions and beliefs coming from the remote past. In fact, Australia has been populated more than 50,000 years ago, which makes the local cultures some of the most ancient in the world.

NEVER SAY GOODBYE

We left Australia in a sunny and warm summer day, heading towards Europe covered by snow. After a year full of adventures we decided to move again. It was a 36-hours flight, with several changes of airlines. First, we went from Hobart to Melbourne by an internal flight with Qantas /the Australian airline/. In Melbourne we got terrified when were told that we needed to throw away half of our luggage because it exceeded the international flights allowances. No option to pay for the excess luggage existed- those are long flights over the ocean and they must not be overloaded. Therefore, the luggage restrictions are severe.

We flew from Melbourne to Singapore where needed to change the airline and to get our tickets validated. If you ever fly via Singapore, you have to calculate at least 4 hours stay there because of the long queues at the desks of the airlines.

Europe welcomed us with snow and freezing winter conditions. People were staring at us while we were walking across Zurich airport in shorts and sandals, waiting for our connection flight.

We spent a year in two Australian states- Tasmania and Western Australia /region of Pilbara/. Both are considered rural places with low level of population. Modern civilization has not destructed them yet, so people who live there can enjoy a peaceful and happy lifestyle, close to the nature. Next time I am planning to visit Queensland- the Promised Land/ and the mythical Northern Territory where crocodiles are wandering in the streets. Australia is a magic place which would not allow people to leave it forever.

www.ingramcontent.com/pod-product-compliance
Lightning Source LLC
Chambersburg PA
CBHW051425250726
48655CB00003B/1244